9 Lies

That Control Our Lives

Miles Edward Allen

Dedication
To Donna, Patrick, and Phyllis

Books by Miles Edward Allen

The Religion of the Future
2023

The Hereafter Trilogy
2015

The Realities of Heaven
2014

Defending Reincarnation
2013

The Afterlife Confirmed:
2012

Games People Actually Play
2011

Christmas Lore & Legend . . . The Game
2009

The Survival Files:
2007

✶ *Religions were created to control people and nations when armies failed, and fear was the tool that kept them in line. If you take the divinity out of any man — take God out of him — then you can easily rule and control him.*
— J.Z. Knight, *Ramtha*, 1986.

Contents

Foreword

Here is the best part,
You'll have a head start,
If you are among the very young at heart.
— "Young at Heart" lyrics by Carolyn Leigh, 1953

I address these writings to the young men and women of the world — generally those between 12 and 22 years of age — because only the young at heart are likely to be receptive to unfamiliar truths. I have no motivation to bolster those who already agree with me, although they may find this book useful (if not entertaining); while those of advanced age who disagree are unlikely to be capable of overcoming the lies that our leaders have worked so hard to ingrain within them.

And so, it is the youth — of this and ensuing generations — upon whom I pin my hopes that someday these lies will prompt the same bewilderment that we now feel about such ancient beliefs as that disease is caused by demons and lightning bolts are thrown by Thor.

The Lies

The nine lies described in this book are untruths that have corrupted civilization, stifled creativity, encouraged fear, and ruined lives for millennia. These have proven to be major stumbling blocks to the achievement of progress, peace, and human dignity. The goal of this book is to expose these lies and free mankind from their bonds.

The Spirit Component

The public's acceptance of most of these lies depends on distortions and misconceptions about what happens to people after death. Understanding that the human personality does, indeed, survive the demise of the physical body is key to realizing truth.

If you doubt the existence of an afterlife, you will benefit from studying the evidence presented in my book, *The Hereafter Trilogy*, and other sources listed in Appendices 2 and 3.

Throughout this book, I have inserted quotes taken from communications between discarnate entities (spirits) and living humans. All statements about characteristics of spirits and conditions extant in the afterlife are derived from the testimony of discarnate souls. See the book, *The Realities of Heaven: Fifty Spirits Describe Your Future Home*, for details.

Those readers who fear that talking to spirits could be sinful should read the discussion of Lie #9 before continuing from here.

With a couple of exceptions, this book consists of essays I wrote between 1997 and 2017.

—Miles Edward Allen
Millsboro, Delaware
29 June 2023

Lie #1: "The physical is inferior."

*Pornographic novels were novels about the
things primates enjoy most, namely sexual acro-
batics. They were taught to feel ashamed of these
natural primate impulses so that they would be
guilty-furtive-submissive types and easy for the
alpha males to manipulate.*
— Robert Anton Wilson, *Schrödinger's Cat Trilogy*,
1988.

People who think of heaven (or some sort of astral plane) generally think of it as a more important, more holy, realm than their current, physical one. A common view is that the Earth plane is a lower, de-graded place, perhaps actually an evil place. A common view, but baseless.

It is not true that the material world is inherently inferior to the spirit realms. The Creating Conscious-ness expresses itself in a myriad of ways; the physical universe being one of them. Planes of existence vary in function and structure, but each is a part of the whole of creation, no part of which is finer or denser, or better or worse, or higher or lower than any other part. To doubt that is to judge the Creator; a risky action at best.

The material world is simply one of the latest expressions of the Great Spirit — the newest (perhaps) resort in which spirits can play! This applies to things such as tables and chairs, flowers and sunsets, and most especially, to our human bodies. Therefore, life in our physical bodies is to be appreciated, explored, enjoyed, and revered as much as life in any heaven.

Note that this does not mean "anything goes." Playfulness never involves coercion. The universal virtues of compassion, tolerance, forgiveness, integrity, and respect should guide all activity in every realm of being.

The lie of corporeal corruption introduced priests and politicians to the idea of shame, a weapon they have wielded for millennia with catastrophic results for the minds and institutions of man. The text below explains some of the dangers of thinking that our physical bodies are intrinsically flawed. This is followed by a rather alarming look at the way women have been held responsible for this supposed inferiority.

A Powerful Shame

Sexologist, Dr. Marty Klein, has written a critically important — and highly recommended — book titled:

America's War on Sex. Any student of the history of religion is aware, however, that that war started long before the 13 colonies got their act together in 1776. The question is: why has such an essential and pleasurable activity been so widely considered something to hide, something to cause shame? The answer, I concluded 40-some years ago,[1] can be found in the world of politics.

Ongoing competitions for dominance are pervasive in the governing structures of most mammalian species — someone always has to be "top dog" and boss everyone else around. Wolves and pumas and puppies and such have a limited repertoire of control techniques; stronger jaws and quicker claws are about all that one can employ to dominate another. We humans are way different. Early on, we exceeded all other life forms in devising methods to gain and exert control over one another.

Even back when humans lived in small tribes, searching the jungle for anything they might eat, or that might eat them, aggression and strength were not sufficient for maintaining power. No matter how tough you were when you took over the tribe, inevitably some young buck would come along and kick your butt out. It is not unreasonable to assume that the smartest chiefs quickly learned to postpone such involuntary retirement by controlling their tribes in other ways.

The way to get people to follow your commands is to constrain their ability to do something important to them. If you could, for example, ration the world's air supply so that everyone had to please you in order to breathe, then your power would be beyond calculation. This, of course, is because air is mankind's most critical natural need. Next in line is water, then food, and then a bunch of social and self-esteem needs, many of which involve sex.

Tribal chiefs couldn't control the world's air supply (although they might have forced the disfavored to sleep near the less fragrant sections of camp). Water and food, being available most everywhere, proved tough to commandeer (at least until agriculture was invented and some chieftain had the nefarious notion that the land itself could be "owned").

Upon first consideration, controlling sexuality might seem a daunting task, after all, social interactions are not commodities that can be monopolized or restricted. Folks are going to follow their urges, despite the urging of their leaders. Yet humans are endlessly inventive, especially when it comes to lording it over other humans. So, it likely didn't take too long for leaders to discover that the key to keeping their subjects submissive wasn't to prevent them from doing this or that, but to make them believe that doing this or that was shameful. Most folks call this practice "religion" but it's really just sexual politics.

Politics is the craft of gaining and maintaining power over others. One of the most effective ways to do that is to utilize the coercive power of shame. Here's why:

Shame lowers self-image, thus giving a relatively higher image to the leader. "The worse I look to myself, the better the chief looks."

Shame helps convince people to accept their lot in life. "I have bad thoughts, so I am a bad person, and I deserve to be treated poorly by the boss."

Shame is a feeling of wrongness that spreads throughout one's psyche and undermines confidence. "If I'm wrong about this, I might be wrong about that, so I should not question my leaders."

Shame causes confusion and uncertainty. "I don't even know how I got so sinful. How can I be sure that any solution or program is good or bad? Who am I to make value judgements?"

Shame promotes feelings of impotency. "My inability to overcome my sinful nature shows that I am weak, proving that I don't have the strength to fight the system successfully."

Shame inhibits the interpersonal communication necessary to resist tyranny. "I don't want people to notice me because they might notice my perversion, so I won't speak out to protect my rights."

Shame leads to isolation, so there is no strength in numbers. "If I join this organization or movement, my guilt may become known, so I'll just keep to myself."

"For women, the very consciousness of their own nature must evoke feelings of shame."
—Saint Clement of Alexandria, Christian theologian
(c150-215) *Pedagogues II*, 33, 2

In summary, people who are ashamed of their own actions, urges, or fantasies, can be uncertain, vulnerable, compliant, and isolated; making them more easily manipulated, misled, intimidated, and impoverished. Consequently, dictators, priests, and other sorts of tyrants work long and hard to convince each and every one of us that we should be ashamed of our bodies, of our desires, of our fantasies, of our very selves.

It's All Her Fault

Few civilized people would concur with the idea that women are inherently inferior to men. But a vast inequality of gender was once deemed to be an obvious truth, and the aftereffects of that belief still have negative impacts on our society. The arguments against this lie hardly need repeating here. The quotes below from influential people (some pretty recent) may help explain why the idea of female inferiority is taking so long to erase from the public consciousness.

In large measure, the attitudes expressed here were founded on the biblical story of Adam and Eve. The idea being that Eve, having been created as his helpmate, led Adam to disobey God, thus bringing about every nasty thing from death to halitosis. (For insight into that misunderstanding, see Lie #5: "Mankind requires salvation.") Farther along in the Old Testament one can find numerous horrific tales that demonstrate the Jewish attitude towards women.

Good Christian Women

It is the Christians, however, who have perfected the vile art of scapegoating women.

> *"If a woman will not veil herself, then she should cut off her hair; but if it is disgraceful for a woman to be shorn or shaven, let her wear a veil. For a man ought not to cover his head, since he is the image and glory of God; but woman is the glory of man. For man was not made from woman, but woman from man."*
> — The apostle Paul, *1 Corinthians* 11:6-8

> *"The women should keep silence in the churches. For they are not permitted to speak, but should*

be subordinate, as even the law says. If there is anything they desire to know, let them ask their husbands at home. For it is shameful for a woman to speak in church."
— The apostle Paul, *1 Corinthians* 14:34-35

"Let a woman learn in silence with all submissiveness. I permit no woman to teach or to have authority over men; she is to keep silent. For Adam was formed first, then Eve; and Adam was not deceived, but the woman was deceived and became a transgressor."
— The apostle Paul, *1 Timothy* 2:11-13

"In pain shall you bring forth children, woman, and you shall turn to your husband and he shall rule over you. And do you not know that you are Eve? God's sentence hangs still over all your sex and His punishment weighs down upon you. You are the devil's gateway; you are she who first violated the forbidden tree and broke the law of God. It was you who coaxed your way around him whom the devil had not the force to attack. ... Woman, you are the gate to hell."
—Tertullian, the "father of Latin Christianity" (c160-225)

"Woman is a temple built over a sewer."
—Tertullian

"Hurtful are women ... the angel of God told me that women are overcome by the spirit of fornication more than men, and they devise in their

*heart against men; and by means of their adorn-
ment they deceive first their minds, and instill
the poison by the glance of their eye. ... Therefore, flee fornication my children, and command
your wives and your daughters that they adorn
not their heads and their faces; because every
woman who acts deceitfully in these things hath
been reserved to everlasting punishment."*
— The Testament of Reuben, circa 3rd century

*"Woman does not possess the image of God in
herself but only when taken together with the
male who is her head, so that the whole substance
is one image. But when she is assigned the role
as helpmate, a function that pertains to her
alone, then she is not the image of God. But as
far as the man is concerned, he is by himself
alone the image of God just as fully and completely as when he and the woman are joined together into one."*
—Saint Augustine, Bishop of Hippo Regius (354-430)

*"Woman is a misbegotten man and has a faulty
and defective nature in comparison to his. Therefore, she is unsure in herself. What she cannot
get, she seeks to obtain through lying and diabol-
ical deceptions. And so, to put it briefly, one
must be on one's guard with every woman, as if
she were a poisonous snake and the horned devil.
... Thus, in evil and perverse doings woman is
cleverer, that is, slyer, than man. Her feelings*

drive woman toward every evil, just as reason impels man toward all good."
—Saint Albertus Magnus, Dominican theologian, 13th century

"As regards the individual nature, woman is defective and misbegotten, for the active force in the male seed tends to the production of a perfect likeness in the masculine sex; while the production of woman comes from a defect in the active force or from some material indisposition, or even from some external influence."
—Thomas Aquinas, Doctor of the Church, 13th century

"For good order would have been wanting in the human family if some were not governed by others wiser than themselves. So by such a kind of subjection woman is naturally subject to man, because in man the discretion of reason predominates."
— Aquinas

"The word and works of God is quite clear, that women were made either to be wives or prostitutes."

"No gown worse becomes a woman than the desire to be wise."

"Men have broad and large chests, and small narrow hips, and more understanding than women, who have but small and narrow breasts, and broad hips, to the end they should remain at

home, sit still, keep house, and bear and bring up children."

"Girls begin to talk and to stand on their feet sooner than boys because weeds always grow more quickly than good crops."

— Martin Luther, Reformer (1483-1546)

"Woman, who by nature (that is, by the ordinary law of God) is formed to obey. The government of women has always been regarded by all wise persons as a monstrous thing. … Now Moses shows that the woman was created afterwards, in order that she might be a kind of appendage to the man; and that she was joined to the man on the express condition, that she should be at hand to render obedience to him."

"Unquestionably, wherever even natural propriety has been maintained, women have in all ages been excluded from the public management of affairs. It is the dictate of common sense, that female government is improper and unseemly."
— John Calvin, Reformer (1509-1564)

"Such be all women, compared to man in bearing of authority: For their sight … is but blindness; their strength, weakness; their counsel, foolishness; and judgement, fantasy."
— John Knox, The First Blast of the Trumpet Against the Monstruous Regiment [unnatural rule] of Women, 1558

"The very being or legal existence of the woman is suspended during the marriage . . . for this reason a man cannot grant anything to his wife or enter into any covenant with her: for the grant would be to presuppose her separate existence, and to covenant with her would be only to covenant with himself."
— Sir William Blackstone, 18th century jurist

"The root of masculine is stronger, and of feminine weaker. The sun is a governing planet to certain planets, while the moon borrows her light from the sun, and is less or weaker."
—Joseph Smith, founder of LDS movement [Mormons] (1805-1844)

"Women are made to be led, and counseled, and directed."
— Heber C. Kimball, LDS apostle (1801-1868)

"A wife is to submit graciously to the servant leadership of her husband, even as the church willingly submits to the headship of Christ."
— Official statement of Southern Baptist Convention, summer 1998

"The feminist agenda is not about equal rights for women. It is about a socialist, anti-family political movement that encourages women to leave their husbands, kill their children, practice witchcraft, destroy capitalism and become lesbians."
— Pat Robertson, Southern Baptist leader

"Women will be saved by going back to that role that God has chosen for them. Ladies, if the hair on the back of your neck stands up it is because you are fighting your role in the scripture."
— Mark Driscoll, preacher, circa 2001

"The Holiness of God is not evidenced in women when they are brash, brassy, boisterous, brazen, head-strong, strong-willed, loud-mouthed, overly-talkative, having to have the last word, challenging, controlling, manipulative, critical, conceited, arrogant, aggressive, assertive, strident, interruptive, undisciplined, insubordinate, disruptive, dominating, domineering, or clamoring for power. Rather, women accept God's holy order and character by being humbly and unobtrusively respectful and receptive in functional subordination to God, church leadership, and husbands."
— James Fowler, *Women in the Church*, 1999

In Summary

"To read the early Church Fathers is to feel some-times that they had never heard of the Nazarene, except as a peg on which to hang their own tor-tured diabolism, and as a blank scroll upon which to indite their furious misogyny."
— John Langdon-Davies, *Short History of Women*, 1927

"Religions are not merely belief systems but so-cial institutions whose leaders have always un-derstood how effectively fear, hate, and the assur-ance of racial, national, or sexual superiority—and sex—can be used to define and control a so-ciety. ... Some politicians have long understood that regimenting sexuality is a time-tested way of maintaining moral authority."
— Francine Prose, "The Original Sin," *Lapham's Quarterly*,

Lie #2: "It ain't natural."

⭐ *"An individual's sexual preference should be viewed as neither good nor evil ... Homosexuality, ... is but the sharing of intimacy. The division into male and female created human sexuality, crossing all lines of the experience— including heterosexuality, homosexuality, and bisexuality. Each pattern is equal in the lesson that, in the sexual expression and in the intimacies of human relationship, each individual should be balanced, loving, and altruistic."[2]*

⭐ *"Many people are learning to accept their androgynous natures. Some express it in homosexuality ... [which] in the long run is a healthy statement in your civilization. Ultimately, we are all androgynous."[3]*

⭐ *Homosexuality "is an evolutionary stage of the spirit ... and it is not to be condemned or honored any more than any other physical or spiritual stage. ... If [an] Earth lifetime was homosexual in orientation, it will enter here the same way. ... Whether heterosexual or homosexual in*

> *nature, the soul-level energy and bonding com-*
> *mitment of all couples is totally respected."*[4]

The statements quoted above were received from discarnate spirits communicating through mediums in 1989, 1985, and 2001 respectively. As far as I know, these are the only mentions of homosexuality by spirits yet published in the English language. Considering the utterance of numerous other spirit-communicators over the past century, this "liberal" attitude is not surprising. Few denizens of the heavens express condemnation of physical pleasures. To quote another spirit communicator:

> ★ *"Nothing about your body or its functions is*
> *either dirty or sinful. … Deny your physical*
> *body expression of which it is capable and you*
> *will suffer."*[5]

But, sin or not, aren't lesbians, gays, and swingers performing "unnatural" acts? Numerous self-appointed moralists have claimed that such creativity should be condemned in man because it does not occur in nature. They have been misinformed.

The species that is our closest relative, sharing 98 percent of our DNA, is the bonobo chimpanzee. "Whether females are in estrus or not, male and female bonobos enjoy sex several times a day with an ever-changing array of partners in their close-knit group … If they come across a choice bit of food in their native range in Zaire, and the bonobos are unsure who will get it, they all start having sex. Females grasp each other face to face and rub their vulvas to orgasm. Both sexes gather round and play feelie. Males 'fence' each other with their erect penises. Females fellate males, males perform cunnilingus on females, and males and females have intercourse, often face to face … All of this sex goes on at once, mind you, and afterward the good feeling is so complete that the food is shared with minimum conflict."[6]

Now, some puritanical critics might well try to use these facts to justify their view that freely practiced sexuality is "animalistic" or "beastly." The reverse is true. Although such practices among some primates do demonstrate that homosexual and multi-sexual activities are not "crimes against nature," neither are they common in the animal kingdom. Thousands of species only interact sexually when pregnancy is possible, while just two enjoy sex without reproducing. It would seem that "sex done purely for pleasure with a variety of partners is actually *more* human than it is animal."[7]

Well then, what about "Thou shalt not commit adultery"? This prohibition originally meant only that a man's wife, being his property, was prohibited from enjoying another man sexually. The tribesmen who came up with this idea never intended to prohibit themselves from having all the wives and mistresses they could afford, while raping any women who had the misfortune of getting in the way of their armies.

Although still a legal matter in most locales, adultery is a null concept for independent people. Afterall, most mammalian creatures are not monogamous. Dogs and cats, horses and cows, monkeys and — most definitely — humans, will have sex with each other whenever an attractive partner is present, and wherever the situation allows[8]. But, "cheating," or betraying the trust of one's spouse, is definitely verboten no matter what dimension one calls home. This is why so many folks have taken up the practice commonly called "swinging." When done correctly, swinging can provide a healthy outlet for urges that matrimony doesn't, while strengthening the marriage bond.

A careful reading of more than 50 books containing descriptions and advice from discarnate spirits has revealed no commentaries on the morality or advisability of participating in group sex, orgies, swinging, or other such revelry. This can't be the result of a lack of experience on the spirit's part, as such goings-on have been going on since they became possible.

Whatever the case, we can confidently conclude that intimate activities occurring among however many people of whichever gender and in whatever formation are altogether natural and fine, providing that the result is pleasing to every soul involved.

Free Love?

This seems a good time to explain an often-misunderstood concept. "Free love" is not a synonym for promiscuity. It does not mean having sex with anyone and everyone. Free love is love free of outside restrictions. That is, no laws or restrictions (by government, religion, or custom) saying physical intimacy can only be enjoyed with particular people, in specified ways, and/or under stipulated conditions — such as between married people of opposite gender, with the lights turned off.

This freedom is constantly under attack from religious fundamentalists, self-appointed moralists, and unprincipled politicians.[9] As with freedom of speech, constant vigilance is required from all citizens.

Only You

The naturalness and goodness of pleasurable sexual activity equally applies when there is but a single person involved.

Most people, even those who were spared a Catholic education, grew up with some feelings that masturbation was wrong. The mere touching of one's body in "certain places" is forbidden in public (for all except major-league baseball players, it seems). Isn't that strange? I can stand anywhere upon the world's stage and rub my elbow or tweak my earlobe without a bit of controversy, but heaven help me should my hand wander down to the area of my greatest pleasure.

This prohibition is rooted, of course, in the general disapproval of pleasure that began with St. Paul and reached a crescendo under Luther, Calvin, and the Puritans. [See Lie #1.] The specific condemnation of masturbation, however, comes from an older source; or, rather, a misunderstanding of an older source.

The ancient Jews had a practice known as a "levirate marriage," which was intended to ensure lineage and property rights in cases where a man died before he had fathered a son. The custom said it was the responsibility of the dead man's brother to inseminate the widow. Chapter 38 of the book of *Genesis* relates the tale of Onan, brother of Er, who was instructed by his father to fulfill his duty to his brother by entering into a levirate marriage with Er's widow, Tamar. But Onan, although no doubt enjoying the (otherwise prohibited) intercourse with Tamar, withdrew before ejaculating and "spilled his seed upon the ground." The assumption being that he did so to prevent the conception of a son, and thus improve his prospects of receiving Er's share of their father's legacy. (Females not being qualified to inherit.) This act, not masturbation,[10] earned Onan the wrath of the Lord.

The founding fathers of the Christian church found it useful to hold up Onan as an example of the wages of fleshly sin, although they usually avoided mentioning the details concerning his attempt to steal Tamar's inheritance. And so, the guilt of Onan has been laid on the shoulders (or the genitals) of every person, male and female, young and old, who has discovered the god-given joys of self-stimulation.

The real shame is shame itself.

Your Natural Self

✸ *"Truly advanced souls have balanced gender preferences in their physical life choices."*[11]

At some point after the death of your physical vehicle, your spirit will make a decision as to whether or not another physical life on Earth is desirable. If the decision is yes, there will be many associated decisions that must be made concerning where, with whom, and as what, you will be born. If you died by accident, you might make these decisions almost instantaneously but, in most cases, you will carefully plan your future life, taking many factors into consideration. Often, you will avail yourself of the assistance offered by spirits you view as having more experience and greater wisdom than you.[12]

Although no spirit is omniscient, no planning process is impervious to error, and sometimes first choices are not available, generally spirits find their new life on Earth to be pretty much what they had chosen prior to birth. The environs and conditions a newly arrived spirit finds itself in are neither decreed nor immutable. Often such seemingly negative choices as poverty or bodily deformities are chosen either as learning opportunities, challenges to be overcome, or to provide another person with a chance to be altruistic.

Whether or not these lessons are learned and the challenges overcome is a matter of the spirit's character and the exercise of its freewill. Nevertheless, there are certain parameters that cannot be altered once the birth is accomplished. These include the location of one's birth, the identity of one's parents, one's race and ethnicity, and one's gender.

It is the latter parameter that recent events call into question. And, although the idea of an "adult male predator in the little girl's room" is a baseless scare tactic, there are some aspects of the transgender controversy that do require thoughtful resolution, particularly in the areas of health, safety, and societal acceptance. On a personal level, there is one question that has not yet gained prominence: What insight can be gained by viewing transgender-related issues through the lens of reincarnation?

Is the pre-birth choice of gender ever made lightly or without much thought? Could a well-considered choice be a mistake? Can the process of selecting the new body malfunction? All these might possibly occur, but extremely rarely — certainly not as often as it seems that folk express dissatisfaction with the result.

Why such dissatisfaction exists may very well be that the spirit is attempting to experience being the opposite gender from that which the spirit was during its most recent lives. We all can change our conditions from one life to the next: from rich to poor, master to serf, gay to straight, black to white to brown to red, and so on. If we have completed a series of lives as female, and chose to be male in the current one, it is understandable that we feel like strangers in our new bodies. But feeling like you are in unfamiliar territory doesn't mean you aren't meant to be there; or that you shouldn't try to make accommodations with the new and get comfortable with who you are now.

Your gender was almost certainly not an accident of nature. In all likelihood, if you were born with (or without) male genitalia, you made a conscious, reasonable decision to live your life in that condition. Before choosing to countermand that decision and change that condition, realize that you were responsible for it.

To change gender post-birth is not a sin, but the act could negate a good deal of previous planning and effort on your part.

Know that, when this life is concluded, you will judge yourself on how well you met the challenges you set for it.

Lie #3: "Virginity is a sacred state."

*Those who can make you believe absurdities; can
make you commit atrocities.*
— Voltaire, Miracles and Idolatry, 1764

The following is a slightly modified version of an article that I wrote a decade ago. It is presented in the manner that I developed for my book, *The Survival Files*, as a conversation held mostly between myself and a wise mentor. This person does have a name, but all those I knew called him 'sir' and referred to him as 'the Old Man," so I continued that custom. The facts presented here reflect the current consensus of objective biblical scholars (that is, of scholars who seek the truth as opposed to religiously indoctrinated academics who only endeavor to buttress their own beliefs).

This article covers several difficulties with the nativity narrative, but it is the lie about the virgin birth which remains a nefarious influence today.

A Christmas Conversation

Wherein an acolyte and mentor from The Survival Files
meet again at a Christmas party and find themselves leading

an impromptu discussion on the origin and meanings of the stories of Jesus' birth.

His red shirt and black slacks and suspenders made him look even more like Santa Claus than when I had first met him at the New Zealand embassy a little over two years before. Setting a half-consumed cup of eggnog aside and peering over his steel-rimmed glasses, he flashed a hearty grin and waved me to a seat beside his wing-backed chair.

"Welcome young man!" he said. (Such was his stature and longevity in D.C. circles that I could take no offense at being so addressed, despite being well past 40 myself.)

"I wasn't expecting to see you here," I said, though nothing this man did was likely to truly surprise me. "Doesn't seem like Christmas would be your thing."

"Oh, I've always loved Christmastime. Especially when sitting by a glowing fireplace and watching the snow."

I followed his gaze out the front window to the glittering flakes drifting through the lights along N street. "This season certainly can be beautiful in Washington … and a bit treacherous." I said, thinking of my recent hike up two blocks of icy walks from my car. Then again, I was lucky to find a parking space at all in Georgetown on a Saturday night.

"But I was referring more to the religious aspects than the meteorological."

"You think my knowledge of the afterlife would make me immune to the dogmas of man? Well, to some extent that is true, but I've always considered the teachings of Jesus to be superior advice and, just as with Ol' St. Nick, one can surely enjoy traditions without swallowing the myths."

"Are you saying that Christianity is based on myths?" This from a young lady standing nearby who had overheard our conversation.

"Uh, oh," I thought, "now you've done it."

"Christianity is a most complex structure built on a variegated foundation. A social gathering such as this is hardly the appropriate place to exhume that foundation, even if I were prone to do so. But, since we are, at least to some extent, celebrating the birth of Jesus with a tree topped by a star and sheltering a creche full of peasants and royalty, perhaps a few words as to how we came by these traditions *would* be appropriate."

With a smile that would disarm a Mormon at a brewers' convention he softly said: "Pull up a seat, I beg you madam, and tell me about the Christmas of your childhood."

"Oh, well, I guess it was pretty much the typical things, you know," she mumbled as she blushed a bit and sat down on the couch opposite us. Her name, she said, was Angela. "We put up the tree a week or so before hand, opened one present on Christmas eve, went to church in the morning … ."

Somewhere during her description of the Christmas feast, I drifted off into memories of my own childhood … the American Flyer train puffing oily smoke as it circled the Norway spruce, the smell of cookies just out of the oven, the candies and oranges in our stockings … and I entirely missed the turn of the conversation to the Bible. When I came out of my reverie, I noticed that several others had joined us, and the Old Man was apparently answering a question about when the first nativity stories were written.

"[*The Gospel According to Matthew* was written] sometime between 35 and 45 years after the death of Jesus; or some 65 to 90 years after his nativity. Although *Matthew* is traditionally placed first among the documents of the *New Testament*, Paul wrote his letters decades earlier and *Mark* was the earliest of the four gospels. *Luke* was written a decade or so after *Matthew*. Paul gives no indication of having heard the nativity tales, so at least two or three generations passed between the time the events were said to occur and their being written down.

"As to who the writers were, there are many lengthy articles and documents devoted to answering (or attempting to answer) that question, but no one really knows. There is general agreement that neither of the authors was a witness to the events described or ever met any of the characters in the stories."

"Wasn't Matthew the tax collector?" Angela asked.

"No, the author of *Matthew* was likely not a native of the Israel/Palestine area and was certainly not one of Jesus' disciples."

"A lot of people don't even realize that there are two different accounts of Jesus' birth," I chimed in. "And they aren't all that consistent."

"Other than the basics that Jesus was born of Mary in Bethlehem," he responded, "the stories of *Matthew* and *Luke* actually have very little in common. *Matthew* tells of astrologers seeing a star and giving gifts to the babe — *Luke* tells of shepherds seeing angels."

"Which could both be true," Angela pointed out.

"Yes, possibly," he admitted, then continued, "*Matthew* has the newborn in a house — *Luke* places him in a stable. *Matthew* claims that the family fled from Bethlehem to Egypt in fear for their lives — *Luke* states that they went to Jerusalem to have Jesus circumcised and then went home to Nazareth. This latter contradiction is absolute and cannot be reconciled in any sane manner. One of the stories (at least) is not totally correct."

Noticing the tightness around Angela's mouth, I asked: "What about their historical accuracy?"

"Well," he continued, "neither governments nor historians of the time paid much attention to births, so it is not surprising that there are no records of Jesus' entry into this world. There are, however, several elements of the biblical narratives that have raised serious questions among biblical scholars and dabblers alike. These are the star, the tax (or census), and Herod's bloody reaction."

"Why is the star significant?"

"Many people have tried very hard to find a reasonable celestial explanation for the star that is mentioned in *Matthew* — supernovas, planetary conjunctions, comets, etc. — none of their theories really hold water. And, even though the Romans, the Egyptians, and the Chinese were very good at both watching the heavens and keeping records, no one noted any event that fits the description.

"The astrologers are first quoted as saying that they 'observed the rising of his star.' This sounds very much like a typical astrological reference to a natural movement of the heavens. The ascendant star being given royal significance in the same way that, say, a conjunction of Mars and Neptune might be interpreted as especially ominous. Currently, though, no records have been found indicating that the Persians thought that any particular alignment of heavenly bodies would signify the birth of a new 'king of the Jews.'"

"Why do you call them 'astrologers,' asked Angela, "weren't they three kings from the Orient?"

"No. There's more of song[13] than story in that idea," he said in what seemed to me to be an uncharacteristically curt manner.

I tried to smooth over the moment by asking: "Couldn't the 'star' have been a local event such as a meteor or simply a unique and miraculous phenomenon?"

"Miracles are notoriously tough to disprove, but consider this: If the star was a local phenomenon, how could it have been seen in Persia some 500 miles away? And if it were visible from a great distance (and thus very high), how could anyone tell over what house it stopped?'

"Yes," I mused, "present-day illustrations often picture a celestial light with a tail pointing downward to illuminate the blessed scene. They remind me of drawings showing a UFO shining a brilliant beam upon some isolated shack."

I'm not sure if he was joking when he raised his eyes to the ceiling and murmured: "Of course, we can't entirely rule out that explanation either."

At that point, I called for a break as I hadn't yet found either the bar or the restroom. Such is the old man's magnetism that when I returned, drink in hand, the now even larger group was sitting quietly as if waiting for class to begin.

Falling into the role of teacher's aide, I got the discussion back in gear by asking, "Why is Luke's taxation/census a problem?"

"Four reasons," he began. "First, because there is no record that Caesar Augustus, or any other Roman dignitary ever issued such a decree, and the Roman bureaucracy kept good records of matters concerning money.

"Second, because the governor named in the story [Quirinius] was not appointed until after Herod's death."

"Another good argument against those who claim that the Bible is always right," I interjected.

"Yes, but there are much better ones and I'm not going to get into all that tonight.

"The third problem with the tax story is that uprooting families all over the province and having them all travel simultaneously to the paternal birthplace would be economically disruptive and politically impossible, not to mention unnecessary and downright stupid. When you take a census, you send the census takers to the people, you don't have the people come to the census takers."

He paused to sip from his cup, and I took the opportunity to add: "Especially when transportation was slow and difficult."

"Exactly. Which brings us to the fourth problem. In the event that such an insanity did take place, only men would need to take part because wives in Judea neither voted nor paid taxes." He looked squarely at Angela and asked: "Are we to assume that Joseph put his about-to-give-birth wife on a donkey and traveled over 100 miles from Nazareth to Bethlehem just because he enjoyed her company?"

At that thought, I noticed that several women in the company seemed to lose the glow of the holiday spirits they had consumed. I said, "Even in the super-patriarchal, women-are-property culture of ancient Palestine, no man would risk the life of a coming child in such a reckless action."

He nodded, "Especially if that man had been told that the child was male."

We all considered that idea for a moment, and then Angela, in a rather subdued voice said, "Okay, so what's wrong with Matthew's story of Herod?"

"Ah that," he sighed. "One of the most tragic stories in the Bible is of King Herod ordering the killing of all the infants in Bethlehem."

I was surprised to hear a new voice: "When Herod saw how the astrologers had tricked him, he fell into a passion, and gave orders for the massacre of all children in Bethlehem and its neighborhood." Someone had found a Bible on a nearby bookshelf and was reading the relevant passage from *Matthew*.

"Fortunately for the children of Bethlehem, and for all of humanity, that tale is one of the most clearly fictitious in the Bible. Herod was despised by the great majority of his subjects. Historians of the time took great care to document his every evil deed — and there were enough to fill volumes. Yet in all the records of Herod's crimes, both petty and terrible, there is not one mention of any such murderous decree.[14] It is simply inconceivable that none of Herod's legion of enemies bothered to take note of such a barbarity."

"Sort of like condemning Hitler for being a tyrant without mentioning the war or the Holocaust."

"Yes. And, even if you could conceive of such an oversight, there is no way that any king (even a beloved one) could get away with murdering the newborn sons of everyone — including merchants, princes, soldiers, generals, priests, etc. — residing in a city."

"But, why would Matthew and Luke make up all those strange events?" (I knew the answer, but I sensed he was waiting to be asked.)

"Quite simply, because their audiences expected it.

"The author of *Matthew* was a scribe who identified strongly with his Jewish heritage. He wrote his story to convince Jews that Jesus was the fulfillment of their messianic expectations. He included lots of miraculous events that his Jewish readers would understand as a drawing of parallels to earlier scripture. He was thereby saying something about the character of Jesus rather than giving a factual history."

"Such as?"

"Well, the tale of Herod's slaughter of newborns was meant to evoke images of the Egyptian Pharaoh seeking to kill the infant Moses; thus linking Jesus and Moses in the readers' minds."

"And what audience was Luke aimed at?" I continued to feed him questions.

"The author of *Luke* was a gentile who wrote to convince the Romans that Christianity was a natural outgrowth of an accepted and law-abiding religion (Judaism) that included all peoples – as opposed to a dissident cult whose members should be fed to the lions. By the time he was compiling his tale, the story had spread that Jesus was a Galilean, whereas the ancient scriptures suggested that a legitimate messiah should be born in Bethlehem. So, 'Luke' probably invented the taxation decree both as a device to have Jesus born in Bethlehem and to demonstrate that the family of his hero was obedient to Roman law.

"Both writers took much of their tale from other traditions known throughout the world."

"You mean like Mary being a virgin?"

He shook his head slightly and spoke as if to clarify my comment. "The <u>divine insemination</u> of Mary is a prime example of this. Being fathered by a god used to be an almost universal qualification for saviors and other great men. Prior to Jesus, those said to be so favored included Plato, Alexander the Great, Caesar Augustus, and Genghis Khan.[15]"

"I once heard that there was a Greek king who responded to the many claims of godly insemination by decreeing the death of any woman who offered such an insult to a deity."

"Yes, I have heard of that also, he nodded. Well, Greece did have a reputation as the god-copulating capital of the ancient world.

"But," he continued, "being impregnated by a god did not typically require one to be a virgin. That little twist to the story apparently stems from the fact that the author of *Matthew* could read Greek but not Hebrew. In an attempt to show that Jesus' birth was the fulfillment of prophecy, Matthew cites a passage from the book of Isaiah. The Greek version of the scripture that he referenced, however, inaccurately read 'Behold a virgin shall conceive …' The original Hebrew text actually reads 'Behold a young woman shall conceive …' This mistake was recognized long ago, but don't expect the Catholic church to start building shrines to 'the young woman Mary' anytime soon."

"You mean that the whole virginity thing," gasped Angela, "the sin, the shame, the repression, the guilt, started because some translator goofed?!"

"Unfortunately, sometimes the devil really *is* in the details." Picking up his now empty cup he asked, "Shall we get some refills and try and regain the festive spirit?"

But, before he could rise, the man holding the Bible got in one last question. "Aren't there other stories of Jesus' birth?"

"Yes, several books telling of the birth and early life of Jesus did not make it through the selection process that took place in the late 4th century. The early church leaders wanted to have four gospels because they believed there were four winds and the Holy Spirit was thought to be embodied in the wind. Some candidates were judged supplementary and some were rejected because they contradicted the ones chosen in matters of doctrine. Some, such as the book called "Infancy II" were likely rejected because they painted a less than flattering picture of Jesus. For example, in one scene, a boy running through the streets brushes against Jesus' shoulder, whereupon Jesus strikes him dead; and, when witnesses complain, Jesus causes them all to go blind.

"Although the older scriptures are chock full of vengeance and mayhem, those who compiled the New Testament were trying to underpin a more compassionate doctrine."

And, with that, he stood, took up his cane, and headed for the refreshment table.

* * *

Later, when I suggested that I might publish this conversation, the old man wrote me a note:

"I wouldn't want it thought that I am anti-Christmas or even anti-Christian. Christianity, in its unadulterated form — *Pure Christianity* — one might say, teaches us to be compassionate, tolerant, and, most of all, forgiving people. I emphatically endorse such high ideals. Whether or not certain myths associated with Christianity have any basis in fact does not, in my opinion, detract from those laudable teachings." — D.W.

Virgin Commentary

Biblical Virgins

According to Bishop Spong, "The understanding of 'virgin' is present only in the Greek word *parthenos*, used to translate the Hebrew word *'almah* in a Greek version of the Hebrew Scriptures. The Hebrew word for virgin is *betulah*. *'Almah* never means 'virgin' in Hebrew."[16] The passage in Isaiah that Matthew cites in his nativity narrative makes no mention of virginity.

Jewish attitudes towards virginity were largely concerned with protecting a father's or future husband's investment in their "property." The Catholic's later adopted the view that physical virginity was most important as an indication of a woman's marriage "to Christ."

To This Day

In contemporary America, numerous organizations use this lie to promote their anti-freedom agendas. A popular approach is to encourage young people to pledge abstinence from sex until marriage. Large numbers sign up ... few follow up. As sexologist Klein points out: "Kids don't abstain — whether they think sex is dangerous or not; whether they make public pledges or not; whether they think God will be mad at them or not. Over 90 percent of Americans have sex before marriage. The only question is whether they will have it in a physically and emotionally healthy environment. The goal of abstinence programs is to ensure they won't."[17]

Lie #4: "The Devil made you do it."

*"I instantly opened my bag, and took out the top
publication. It proved to be an early edition—
only the twenty-fifth — of the famous anony-
mous work (believed to be by precious Miss Bel-
lows), entitled The Serpent at Home. The design
of the book — with which the worldly reader
may not be acquainted — is to show how the
Evil One lies in wait for us in all the most apparently innocent actions of our daily lives. The
chapters best adapted to female perusal are 'Satan in the Hair Brush'; 'Satan behind the Look-
ing Glass'; 'Satan under the Tea Table'; 'Satan
out of the Window'; and many others."*
—Drusilla Clack, a character in *The Moonstone*
by Wilkie Collins, 1868.

In 1970, comedian Flip Wilson popularized the character Geraldine Jones whose catch phrase "The Devil
made me do it!" is often repeated to this day. Although
that phrase is usually tossed off in a joking manner, the
idea of satanic influence in human affairs is no laugh-
ing matter. As the ultimate bogyman, the image of a

King of Hell is employed to terrify the ignorant and the weak-minded into submitting to the will of tyrants and Bible salesmen throughout Western culture.

Since the dawn of civilization in Sumer,[18] most religions/myths portray the evil doer as a rebel or disobedient character (angel or man) who violates some divine directive, thus assuming a combative relationship with the higher powers. Surprisingly, an exception to the bad boy as adversary is the religious book most associated with tales of horror and mayhem — the so-called "Old Testament."

Ask the typical churchgoer: "When does the Devil first appear in the Bible?" and their most likely response will be some part of the *Genesis* story of the Garden of Eden. They will usually be surprised to learn (assuming that they are open to learning) that the Devil, as we have come to know him, is not mentioned anywhere in the Old Testament.

The book of Genesis speaks only of a serpent, a symbol of wisdom throughout many cultures. (Check out the Caduceus and the Staff of Asclepius.) His role in the story is more of a quality-control officer, sent by Jehovah to evaluate the reliability of the new creations. The serpent is subtle, but honest; telling only the truth about what will happen when Adam and Eve eat of the tree of the Knowledge of Good and Evil.

The Satan so prominent in the book of *Job* is more of a prosecuting attorney charged with testing Jehovah's creations, he is given no power to wreak havoc on his own. Satan is mentioned, without description or comment, only two other times (*Chronicles* 21:1 and *Zechariah* 3:1-2). The term "demons" likewise only appears twice (Deut 32:17 and Psalms 106:37) and each time seems to be simply another term for false gods that fickle Hebrews were punished for worshiping.

Strange Serpent

What, do you suppose, did the serpent look like *before* it was cursed to crawl on its belly? Did it have legs like a lizard? Wings, like a dragon?

Noting the serpent's wisdom and its ability to talk, some claim that its image is based on a tribal memory of reptilian extra-terrestrials who first brought civilization to primitive man. If several modern authors are to be believed, these beings are still visiting Earth rather frequently, perhaps to check up on their "children." An outrageous idea, but not any stranger that many of the stories in the Bible.

Let's try to keep an open mind.

A Contrived Adversary

As time passed, and as the Jews were exposed to other religions (especially in Babylon) the tempter was seen less as an employee and more as an opponent of Jehovah. Among the Essenes and the followers of Jesus, the figure variously called Satan, Beelzebub, or Belial became a figure of central importance. The authors of *Mark* introduce the Devil into the crucial opening scene of that gospel, and go on to characterize Jesus' ministry as involving "continual struggle between God's spirit and the demons, who belong, apparently, to Satan's `kingdom' (see Mark 3:23-27)."[19]

At the least, this was a significant deviation from mainstream Jewish tradition. To many Jews, this was blasphemy, as it implied that there was more than one god or that their god was not omnipotent.

The Image of Evil

From the first priests on the step pyramids beside the Euphrates river, to the fire breathing preachers in revival tents along the wide Missouri, the personification of evil has almost always been imagined as having horns. Some say these are mimics of goats, some say bulls, others claim extra-terrestrial origins. Current illustrations generally give the Devil and his minions cloven hooves; most likely based on Pan, the half-goat, half-man, Greek god of the wild. As for color, historically the Devil was thought to be black (although Chaucer thought him green). The popularity of a fiery red is fairly recent, but it could have originated with the red dragon mentioned in St. John's bizarre dream known as *The Revelation*.

A Growing Monstrosity

Over the ensuing millennia, Satan became a very definite and prominent figure in Christian dogma, with well-defined habits and intentions. The view developed that he was God's — that is, Christianity's — immortal enemy. As such, he was immensely useful to all who could profit from claiming to fight against him. Vast fortunes have been collected by devious organizations from the trembling masses who hoped their contributions would keep the Devil at bay.

Satan's mission began to be seen as trying to mislead folks into denying or perverting Christian morals and practices. And he did far more then attempt to persuade: "The Devil frequently engaged in those sexual acts that were forbidden to men and women and, in some accounts, he is described as having a forked penis, so that he could commit fornication and sodomy at the same time."[20]

A corollary to this change in the Devil's role — from aide to opposition — was a change in view of the sinner from one who could not resist temptation to one who chose to be in league with Satan, *i.e.*, actually was in opposition to God. As this idea developed further, people began to view their enemies as part of Satan's army.

This often escalated into grand conspiracy theories in which anyone who disagreed with the prevailing view was considered a dangerous enemy manipulated by the Devil. Killing heretics (that is, those who disagreed with you) was therefore not only justified, it was seen as a service to God.

This view is very much extant in today's milieu. "The idea of a tangible satanic force that must be battled out in the world is familiar to tens of millions of fundamentalist and evangelical Christians. At various times, the group said to embody this Evil has been identified as pagans, Jews, Muslims, Catholics, Mormons, and communists. These days they're homosexuals, liberals, and pornographers."[21]

The Spirits' View

Here are a few quotes from those spirits who are most likely to have met the Devil, if he did exist.

> ★ *"Satan is a legend, a story, a fantasy which describes and gives substance to the negative powers of the mind."*[22]

> ★ *"There is no such being as the Devil or Satan or whatever name you give to him. I always liked `Beelzebub.' Satan or the Devil is an invention of man. ... Some religions use it to frighten people into being good, which is self-defeating of itself."*[23]

★ *"The bindings of ignorance, or of the lesser good, may as well be called Satan, or Lucifer. Whatever name you give it, it is still ignorance. It is still the lesser good."*[24]

★ *"I do not think there is anything corresponding to the Devil of orthodoxy."*[25]

★ *"There is no evil except that which we create, for I have seen no signs of a devil on this side of the veil. We are our own devils, with our thoughts and subsequent deeds."*[26]

★ *"The idea that a King of Evil exists, whose direct function is to oppose the King of Heaven, is stupid; it is primitive and even barbaric. The Devil as a solitary individual does not exist, but an evil soul might be called a devil, and in that case there are many devils."*[27]

Today, reasonable and well-informed people realize that there is no dreadful entity forever plotting to ensnare the unwary in webs of sin and dissolution. The Dark Side of "The Force" is ignorance. But, as Walter M. Miller, Jr. has so eloquently pointed out:

Ignorance is king. Many would not profit by his abdication. Many enrich themselves by means of his dark monarchy. They are his Court, and in his name they defraud and govern, enrich themselves and perpetuate their power.[28]

And so, there is no Devil. We have only ourselves to blame.

But There Are Demons

In later Judaism and Christianity, various lesser demons were described as the members of the Devil's staff of subordinates. Not only were Satan's chief lieutenants given names, the exact number of his army of demons was declared in the Talmud to be 7,405,926.[29]

While religions are way off target regarding the Devil Himself, their view on His minions is somewhat more aligned with reality.

Dying has little or no effect on personalities. People who are compassionate, tolerant, and joyful in life will be kind and playful spirits in the next. Likewise, disoriented, disaffected, or dissatisfied souls will remain so after their physical demise. Of course, they can and do change, grow, and improve their situation; but there are, and have been, so many nasty people on Earth that the number of nasty spirits is immense. It should come as no surprise that many of them do not have the best interests of terrestrial humans at heart.

Here is what a few denizens of the astral plane have to say on the matter:

> ✶ *"Billions of mediocre souls are closest to your
> Earth. The attraction Earth exerts upon these
> souls is amazing and comparable to a magnet."*[30]

✸ *"The heavens above your head now are literally swarming with souls who long to take a hand in the business of Earth, souls who cannot let go, who find the habit of managing other people's affairs a fascinating habit, as enthralling as that of tobacco, or opium."*[31]

✸ *"There are many who do not progress for hundreds and sometimes thousands of years who are still filled with the desires of Earth even when they have passed to the world of spirit."*[32]

✸ *"A number of spirits do live and spend most of their time near the Earth, but they are the very unprogressed and find their pleasures in mingling with mortals."*[33]

✸ *"Countless multitudes of insane, diseased, and ignorant spirits wander around in all directions in the circles closest to the Earth's crust."*[34]

✸ *"The lower astral planes also contain people who have been alcoholics or drug addicts, who find these cravings still with them in the astral bodies. They stay near the Earth to be near alcoholics or drug addicts who are still in the physical body, in order to participate vicariously in the sensations which alcohol and drugs give."*[35]

✸ *"Drunks on this side hover around the Earth souls who drink too much, lusting after the pleasures of alcoholism and unable to break the bond of habit which binds them to physical body."[36]*

★ *"There are weak, malicious spirits here, who have never got beyond an elementary development and who are only capable of mischievous activities. Normally they cannot reach the consciousness of men but when emotional disturbances accompany development they are attracted and will attach themselves so as to influence the person in wrong ways and to accentuate the suffering of both mind and body."[37]*

★ *"I became acquainted with different persons who were endeavouring to continue their physical life. ... some even penetrated to the Earth again. There they caused as much disturbance as they could evilly devise by joining with those of a like mind who were still physical beings. This explains perhaps, why such incomprehensible things are sometimes done by humans who are not capable of controlling their own inclinations."[38]*

Just as you cannot rightfully claim that "the devil made you do it," so trying to shift the blame to nasty spirits cannot relieve you of responsibility for your actions. For a discarnate spirit to influence your mind, he or she must be invited in — either by taking (or suffering) actions that weaken your natural defenses or consciously by attempting to contact the dead without proper training or reasonable precautions.

Using the Talking (Ouija[39]) Board

Of all the diviner's devices, the talking board is the most popular. Perhaps this is because its low cost and ease of use appealed to many who wouldn't think of buying a crystal ball or learning to read tarot cards. Also, using the board is a social thing requiring at least one person and usually two people to touch the traveler and another to copy down the messages being spelled out. Before the advent of horror movies on late-night television, many young folks sought answers to burning questions ("Will I marry a handsome man?" "Does Frankie love me?") from the board. This proved especially thrilling on dark and stormy nights amid flickering candles.

Unfortunately, not all encounters with the powers behind the board have been so innocent or harmless. Many people claim that playing with a talking board can open portals to other dimensions, letting in immoral or amoral spirits who revel in encouraging nasty deeds and may even try to possess the naive planchette pusher. The recommendations made for dealing with such interlopers range from prayer to envisioning white auras to trashing the board altogether.

Nevertheless, the talking board is hugely important because several of the best mediums and channelers employed it to make their initial contact with the spirit realms.

This author would, therefore, advise those trying out the talking board to exercise caution and common sense. Any messages coming through the traveler should be evaluated in the same manner as would commentary or advice received from any other stranger. As the Bible commands, "Do not trust any and every spirit, test the spirits to see whether they are from God."[40]

Lie #5: "Mankind requires salvation."

This may be the most controlling of all these lies, as it takes all power away from the individual and gives it to the church/priest. Essentially, it says that all people were born defective in the eyes of their Creator, and there is nothing they can do on their own to make up for their deficiencies, except to beg forgiveness and do whatever their religion dictates.

Even though it is preposterous on its surface, this lie is so ingrained in our society that its negative influence has continued unabated for many millennia.

The text below sheds some light on the origins of "original sin," and then considers the fruits of our personal transgressions.

The Garden of Delight

Every culture has a creation myth, except the Judeo-Christian culture ... it has two creation myths. The earliest is told in Genesis 2 through 4. The other was picked up later and tacked on to the front of the Old Testament, as Genesis 1.

Some claim, and the ignorant sometimes believe, that the two stories can be reconciled one to the other, but that is impossible. Consider that in the first account

Jehovah made the animals before he made humans (both male and female simultaneously),[41] while in the second account Jehovah is said to have made man (male only) first, then the animals, and then woman.[42]

Both stories contain many outrages to astronomy, biology, and common sense. Nevertheless, the story of Eden in Genesis 2 and 3 is critical to our understanding because it provides the basis for what, in later philosophies, would be called "original sin," and original sin is indispensable to politicians, for without it, we mortals would not be in need of salvation.

Of course, you've known this story since you were a child: Adam and Eve, the only two people on Earth, are living in a beautiful garden that Jehovah had planted for them in Eden. Satan lies to Eve and gets her to disobey Jehovah by eating an apple and sharing it with Adam; Jehovah retaliates by kicking them both out of the garden, thus revoking their immortality and introducing pain, suffering, and death into the world. Right?

Well, sort of right. Let's go over it again, just to clear up a few misconceptions.

After Jehovah has made woman and placed her in the garden with man, we are told that "the man and his wife were both naked, and were not ashamed." To many people today —certainly to the millions of practicing nudists — this seems a pretty silly statement;

why should they be ashamed? But to the ancient Jews who wrote this account, being seen naked was a terrible violation. This is evident in their numerous and strict laws on the subject and is vividly illustrated in the reaction of Noah when he realizes that his adult son has seen him naked.[43] To state that the first humans were not ashamed of being seen naked was the strongest possible way for a Jewish writer to emphasize that the first people on Earth were completely uncivilized, like animals, with no sense of right and wrong.

Next, we are introduced to the serpent, a symbol of wisdom throughout many cultures. Note, that there is no reference to an evil entity; Satan was not invented until early Christians decided that an unholy power was required to explain the presence of evil in the world. Up until then, if there were terrible things to be done, Jehovah was perfectly capable of handling the job himself.

The serpent asks the woman if Jehovah has told her not to eat of any of the trees in the garden. She replies that Jehovah told her not to eat of the tree in the middle of the garden, "lest you die." (Note: the word "apple" does not appear in the story.) The serpent replies: "You will not die. For God knows that when you eat of it your eyes will be opened, and you will be like God, knowing good and evil." The serpent has gotten a lot of bad press for making this statement, and perhaps he deserves some of it, but, in fact, everything he said was true! Neither the man nor the woman died, their eyes were opened, and they did come to know good and evil.

Jehovah becomes very angry when he finds out about this infraction, and he hands out curses all around. The serpent must thereafter crawl on its belly and eat dust. Jehovah says he will "greatly multiply" the woman's pain in childbirth. And he tells the man that he will have to work for a living "until you return to the ground."

And then Jehovah says, "Behold, the man has become like one of us, knowing good and evil; and now, lest he put forth his hand and take also of the tree of life, and eat, and live forever,"[44] He sends Adam and Eve out of the garden. Note here, that there is no indication that Adam and Eve were going to live forever in the garden (and lost their immortality when they got kicked out). In fact, it seems that they were forced to leave precisely to prevent them from becoming immortal (by eating from the tree of life).

There is much high strangeness in this story. What kind of god can't see the man and woman hiding in the garden and has to call out "Where are you?"? How could the pain of childbirth be multiplied when it hadn't been experienced up to that moment? And, most strange, indeed, what is meant by the phrase "become like one of us"? This is carrying the "editorial we" or the "royal we" much too far. Clearly, the reader is to understand that Jehovah is speaking to His peers, whoever they might be.

As interesting as such puzzles are, the overriding question is: What does it mean to eat of the tree of the knowledge of good and evil?

Many people, especially puritanical preachers, have muddied the issue with references to sexuality. This is understandable; if you can't (or don't want to) explain something, just imply that it involves sex and most people won't question you any further on the subject.

But sex is never mentioned in the story. Neither is lust. Or even love. There is no talk about bodily functions or emotional urges at all.

In essence, the story of the Garden of Eden is saying that when humans learn to distinguish between good and evil (that is, when they gain the mental capacity to foresee and evaluate the future impact of their actions), they lose their ability to live as the animals do, free of responsibility, duty, and the burdensome knowledge of their own mortality. In other words, wisdom brings painful awareness of vulnerability (*i.e.*, nakedness) and of death.

Once upon a time, we lived in paradise, blissfully unaware of moral choices, ethical dilemmas, free radicals, and cholesterol. Then we got bitten by the wisdom snake, and we opened our eyes to see the often-troubling consequences of our actions, so we started worrying, and we stopped smelling the roses, and went out to work for our bread.

And what of the pain of childbirth? There is a direct physical link here. Wisdom requires more developed brains, which necessitate larger heads, which stretch the birth canal beyond its design specifications.

Some say this world of trouble is an illusion, caused by our hysterical reaction to the serpent's venomous view of things. Maybe we can achieve paradise once again; maybe we can't. But the point to remember is that the story of the Garden does *not* talk about a "fall of man" or about "original sin"; the politicians didn't think of that concept until centuries later.

Without a generalized, inherent sin, mankind is in no need of universal salvation. It may well be that we can improve our heavenly lot by following the teaching of this or that master; but Adam and Eve's legacy does not burden us with the need to be "saved."

A Sumer Garden[45]

Some 5,700 years ago, civilization sprang up in Sumer, on the plains where the Euphrates and Tigris rivers meet in what is now Iraq. Seemingly from nowhere, great cities appeared with the first known planned streets, irrigation systems, and lush public gardens. When the Sumerians lost their cities to the Akkadians 500 years later, they must have lamented the loss of their glorious gardens on the plain.

In the Sumerian language, the word for "plain" was "eden."

When the Jews of 900 B.C.E. speculated about the origin of mankind ("adam" is Hebrew for "mankind") they wrote that it occurred about 3,000 years previously in a "garden eastward in Eden." In other words, about 600 miles due east of Jerusalem on the plains of Sumer. Coincidently, the word "eden" also happens to be a Hebrew word that means "delight." So, the birthplace of civilized man naturally came to be thought of as a "garden of delight."

Still Responsible

The fact that you were born without some dark stain upon your soul does not mean that the way is clear to do your own sinning without consequence. We are all free to get ourselves into as much trouble as we like.

What, then, is sin? A majority of the followers of the three main western religions would refer to some version of the "Ten Commandments" for guidance on this question, so let's consider a "Cliffs Notes" version of the ten (or nine?[46]) commandments:

1. No other gods
2. No idols
3. No misuse of holy name
4. No work on 7th day
5. Honor dad and mom
6. No killing
7. No adultery
8. No stealing
9. No lying
10. No envy

The first four of these are all about the Jewish priesthood protecting their turf (and their livelihood) from outside competition. This is said to have started some 3,200 years ago when Moses granted his older brother, Aaron, exclusive rights to access Jehovah, and is of no consequence to any truth seeker.

The fifth commandment is rather innocuous — providing, that is, that the parents in question are not irresponsible drug addicts, violent abusers, child pornographers, etc.

The tenth (Thou shalt not covet thy neighbor's whatever.) is one of the earliest examples of a law that is intended to criminalize normal behavior; thus, laying a guilt trip on an entire population.

Commandments 6 thru 9 may seem straightforward and applicable to modern life, until one realizes that their authors meant them in a very restricted and jingoistic way. Lying to foreigners, stealing from Gentiles, killing non-Jewish men, women, and children, were all acts glorified throughout the Old Testament, both before and long after Moses delivered the tablets. And, to men who had multiple wives and concubines, adultery meant using another Jew's property without permission. Raping the women of conquered tribes was both expected and often enjoined.

Altogether, then, we can consign these ancient prohibitions to history's garbage heap and move on to more contemporary sources in our search for the meaning of sin.

On second thought, I'll spare you (and me) the summation of 5 millennia of criminal law, and jump to my favorite definition of sin, as stated by the esteemed author, Robert A. Heinlein: *Sin lies only in hurting other people unnecessarily.*[47] (I would add "knowingly" before "hurting," although I quake at the idea of editing the master.)

To put all this in positive and more relatable wording, the absence of a fundamental sin by our progenitors does not free us of the need to be compassionate, tolerant, respectful, honest, and forgiving in all our dealings with each other.

Conscience Decisions

In the Early 1900s, Aleister Crowley popularized the phrase: "Do what thou wilt is the whole of the law." This is quite dangerous advice, sure to get one in trouble in every realm, *unless* "thou" refers to a person who is in harmony with his or her conscience.

Every soul comes equipped with a conscience, an instinctual understanding/feeling of what is right and wrong, positive and negative. But here, in the physical realm, there are many powers that compete with the urgings of that conscience. The allure of achievement, the call of duty, the drive for dominance, the need for security, the thirst for vengeance, and other such forces can diminish or virtually stifle that "still small voice" that tells us right from wrong.

When someone succumbs to such forces and suppresses or ignores the urgings of their conscience, they may not suffer any ill effects — until, that is, they find themselves free of their animal bodies — then there really can be "hell to pay." This is because the physical brain, by its nature, tends to insulate the residing soul from its conscience and, once physical death has set the mind free from the brain, the soul becomes subject to the perfect memory of its deeds and the full knowledge of its transgressions. Or, to quote Spiritualist philosopher David Gow: "The flames of a materialistic hell-fire are but a pale representation of the pangs of an outraged conscience."[48]

Art Thou God?

Although absolute certainty is elusive, the consensus of those discarnate spirits who ought to know is that each soul is an experiential unit of the Universal Consciousness. That is, a part of God designed to allow God to know Itself.

In the 1970s and 80s, the phrase "Thou art God" was often repeated within the New Age community, even popping up in science fiction best sellers.[49] This meme drew the ire of many who felt their God needed defending — some thought it pantheistic, some blasphemous. They were at least partially correct. Everything is a part of the One, but not necessarily Its entirety. We <u>are</u> God in the same manner that my left index finger is me; but there is much, much more.

Your Inner Honor

What, then, of judgement?

It seems we judge ourselves … but the prosecuting attorneys are legion!

Here are some of the reports we have received:[50]

★ *"If you have done wrong things … your soul will know this. When it returns home, that knowledge will sadden your soul and it will grieve for those wrong things that were done."*[51]

✸ *"Whatever judgment or limitation you place on another, it becomes a law within your own consciousness; and by that law, so shall you be limited, and so shall you judge yourself."*[52]

✸ *"After a period of adjustment or orientation, you begin your evaluation of the physical-life experiences you have just completed. You correlate that with your complete knowledge of all the other experiences you have had throughout all your incarnations. ... You are the sole judge of your growth."*[53]

✸ *"You yourself are judge and jury. ... Self accused, you have no escape."*[54]

✸ *"There is no Great Judge presiding over us here ... Any punishment brought about in your world, but accountable in ours, is paid for solely by the transgressor himself."*[55]

✸ *"What you see about yourself, how far you fell short, and what golden opportunities you failed to use, is heartbreaking. You feel such shame, other times anger."*[56]

✸ *"In this process of recollection, as an incident comes back to one's mind it brings with it the actual feelings, not of oneself alone but of the others who were affected by the event. All their feelings have now to be experienced in oneself as though they were one's own."*[57]

★ *"Consciousness is its own judge. So there must be individual unhappiness until that consciousness is appeased."*[58]

★ *"The impression made upon my mind was that as if all senses had united in one grand effort to place my past life in its true phases before me. I sat appalled and dismayed; and then as the record of weaknesses and failures went on, I covered my face with my hands, and sank in agony and shame to the ground. Truly there is record kept of every event in our lives."*[59]

Note that these scenarios make no allowance for any adherence to creed or holy writ. Protestations of faith cannot impact the judgement process. You can proclaim Jesus or Krishna or Mohammed or whomever as your personal savior just as loudly and publicly as you may be moved to do, and it won't make an iota of difference when you come face to face with your conscience.

The only god that judges you is the part that resides within you.

Do not assume it will forgive and forget.

Lie #6: "You only live once."

The idea of souls living numerous lifetimes in different physical bodies has never been popular with those who seek to control and subjugate the populace via threats of eternal damnation and other fearsome denouements. And so, both Christian and Islamic priests and politicians have long sought to repress belief in reincarnation and promote, instead, the lie that each of us only lives once.

The System of Rebirth

We humans might be tiny parts of our creator, but only those with grossly inflated egos could think that they are capable of comprehending the vastness of Creation, let alone translate it into human language. Recognizing, therefore, that only the Almighty knows the true nature of the soul, we are limited to examining the facts that impact our awareness and making the best guess we can at the truth of the matter. The following is my best guess, based on careful analysis of the information contained within literally hundreds of books about Survival and rebirth.

I am a combination of three things: my consciousness, my memories, and my body.

1. Consciousness: My consciousness is a subset of the Universal Consciousness otherwise known as God, Allah, or whatever name you prefer. The best analogy for this might be a node in a network (or a single computer on the Internet); a recognizably separate entity yet still connected in some way to the whole.

This particular bit of consciousness has been "mine" since it was created (that is, since this tiny part of the network was sectioned off from the central core — perhaps eons ago, perhaps a moment before I awoke on Earth). Just as a computer has programs that interface with the user (such as word processing and games) and other programs that are hidden from the user, so an individual's consciousness is partly focused on the physical world and partly attuned to other realms.

2. Memories: My memories consist of all the information of which my particular bit of conscious has ever become aware. Some of this information, especially that which concerns my current life in the physical, is readily available to my physically focused consciousness. Other memories are normally hidden.

3. Body: My body is the primary mechanism by which my consciousness interacts with the physical world. The critical organ enabling this interaction is my brain — a very sensitive system capable of transforming thought into electronic signals.

When I die, my body disintegrates. The physical particles that constituted it are widely dispersed, some to be incorporated into the bodies of other humans. Therefore, there can be no resurrection of the body and the "I" that was defined, in part, by my body cannot be reborn.

But my consciousness is independent of my body. It does not, it cannot, die — at least not as long as the overall network of which it is a part (*i.e.*, God) continues to exist. And my memories, which are embedded within consciousness, likewise cannot be lost. So, while my body will not survive death, my consciousness and my memories will survive. And, as Meat Loaf points out: two out of three ain't bad. [60]

Reincarnation, therefore, is a process whereby the bit of consciousness that once resided in one physical body (that is now dead) enters into a newly created body. In so doing most of its associated memories are repressed, allowing fresh memories of a new life to be accumulated without being unduly influenced or contaminated by recollections of previous lives.

In a number of instances, for reasons we can only guess at, some of these memories are not entirely blocked; they may be triggered by certain experiences, surface in childhood, or be uncovered during hypnosis.

They may also be revealed via physical effects such as birthmarks and deformities. Though the earlier physical body no longer exists, the memories of that body are retained.

Although a discarnate soul may select its future body (situation, parents, etc.) early on, the consensus of spirit testimony is that the soul does not enter that body (making it a human) until about 2 weeks before or after birth.

Examples

Here are a few brief descriptions of cases examined in the Survival-Top-Forty compendium of reincarnation cases. If that website is unavailable, or if you prefer the book form, the cases may also be found in *Defending Reincarnation*.[61]

One More Mission: Young boy describes events in previous life as fighter pilot in WWII. Christian-fundamentalist father attempts to uncover alternative explanation, ends up amassing overwhelming evidence for reincarnation. [Case #65.]

Round Trip to Allentown: Journalist assigned to write article on past-life therapy discovers his own prior life in a distant state. Details revealed under hypnosis — including soldier's name and dog-tag number — are confirmed by U.S. Department of Defense. [Case #63.]

Submariner Resurfaces: Man finds relief from mysterious pain and phobias when trance reveals his prior death in submarine sinking. Names, boat identifications, names of crew members, and more match Navy archival records. [Case #59.]

The Numbers of the Beast: As a volunteer in a hypnosis demonstration experiences life in Nazi concentration camp, red welts appear on her arm in the form of numbers. The Holocaust Museum in Israel identifies numbers as belonging to a girl perfectly matching the one described by the volunteer. [Case #21.]

The Apprentice Murderer: At different times, two unrelated patients tell of the same murder taking place in the 12th century – one from the murderer's point of view and the other as the victim. Each describes the same uncommon situation and provides the same unusual names. [Case #22.]

What Reincarnation Is Not

Sometimes reincarnation is confused with possession, which is the takeover of a body by a personality that was not born into that body while the original personality seems to step aside. The takeover can be for only a few minutes, or for a few months, or for the remainder of the body's life. (Cases numbered 66, 45, and 71 on the Survival-Top-40 list demonstrate these situations.) If the takeover is for an extended time, it is often continuous but sometimes it is intermittent.

The best way to distinguish between reincarnation and possession is to ascertain if the subject, while exhibiting his or her contemporary personality, has memories (either spontaneously or while hypnotized) of *being* the alternate personality. If so, you are dealing with reincarnation. If, on the other hand, the person only recognizes one life situation at a time, then possession, or something else besides reincarnation, is involved.

Memories of past lives are also confused occasionally with the output of a medium. The two best examples of this are the writings of Pearl Curran and Chico Xavier.[62] But neither ever felt that they *were* the personalities that took control of their hands and wrote literally millions of highly literate and historically accurate words.

Also, reincarnation is not transmigration, which is the movement of a soul between humans and other animals. Although some religions have long taught this idea, we have no good evidence that it ever occurs.

Lie #7: The end justifies the means.

"Now Jesus don't like killin'

No matter what the reason's for,

And your flag decal won't get you

Into Heaven any more."

— John Prine, 1971

Great Britain does not go to heaven. Neither does General Electric Corporation, nor the Presbyterian Church, nor the Green Party. No groups may enter, and no causes either. Only the souls of human beings live on in other realms of glory.

The entrance exam at the Pearly Gates does not cover how well one's favorite football team did last year nor how well one's portfolio did last quarter. There are no qualifications based on what was built, whether sky-scrapers or pyramids; nor on what was accomplished, be it world peace or environmental devastation.

All of which does not mean that one's actions do not matter. Actions matter very much, for they are strong indicators of intent; but the *results* of those actions matter very little. When you look back on your life on Earth, you will feel little or no pride in your material accomplishments, but you will be pleased — or dis-pleased — with the person you have become.

In the end, the only thing that counts is the quality of a person's character. This is evaluated according to how well that person followed his or her conscience. Violating that inherent sense of right and wrong will negatively affect any future verdicts — even when done for "a good cause." This is because causes don't count in heaven. According to a consensus of spirit tes-timony,[63] political arrangements, religious creeds, cul-tural practices, and such, are of no concern in the non-material realms. That means that carnage and/or decep-tion cannot be justified in the name of democracy, or divine dictates, or free health care. Each of the measures one employs to achieve an end must be justi-fiable unto itself, and cannot be defended by the in-tended final result.

The Jesuits were wrong; the end does *not* justify the means.

For example, you might claim that it is okay to in-still fear and mental trauma in school children because you thereby can create disciplined and well-ordered minds which are properly infused with the teaching of mother church. But it is of no matter whether submis-sive and indoctrinated children are a worthy goal or not. Harming children, or anyone, with threats and lies is a violation of conscience and cannot be justified.

The justification for killing can be a bit more complex. Firstly, there is the matter of *who* is being killed. The commandant, "Thou shalt not kill," was written by priests who directed the killing of hundreds of thousands of people with (so they thought) both the blessing and the assistance of their fearsome god. Clearly, that ancient directive only prohibited the killing of fellow Jews. Some claim that it is immoral to kill anything; but I find that view tough to justify in a world where the survival of every animal requires it to kill (or destroy) other living things, be they cabbages or kings or all things in between.

As I understand, it isn't who or what you kill that matters, but why. The operative parameter is motivation. Killing animals for food is okay; killing animals for sport is not. To keep a clear conscience, only the immediate threat of severe injury or death to you or to those within your care is sufficient motivation for killing another person.

The above statement leaves considerable room for interpretation, which I leave to others. My point is that any injurious behavior — be it killing, stealing, fraud, or simply being unkind — cannot be excused by adherence to a faith, allegiance to a country, belief in a principle, or a struggle for justice. When you pass through the door of physical death, your conscience rules supreme, and it judges only on means taken without consideration of ends sought. You cannot hide from your conscience forever, so best be true to it now.

"The ends justify the means" is a most insidious lie which has been used to defend vast numbers of egregious acts both personal and global. It should be challenged and corrected whenever it arises.

Lie #8: Biblical Values are best.

"Whenever we read the obscene stories, the voluptuous debaucheries, the cruel and torturous executions, the unrelenting vindictiveness, with which more than half the Bible is filled, it would be more consistent that we called it the word of a demon, than the word of God. It is a history of wickedness, that has served to corrupt and brutalize mankind ... it is a book of lies, wickedness, and blasphemy; for what can be greater blasphemy than to ascribe the wickedness of man to the orders of the Almighty?"
—Thomas Paine, American Patriot,
The Age of Reason, 1794

These days, we often hear that children must be taught "Biblical Values" and our politics and culture should be grounded in a "Biblical world view." One cannot help but wonder if those promoting such ideas have ever actually read their Bibles! An unbiased look shows us that the Bible endorses, promotes, and often glorifies all of the following undesirable activities.

Genocide

Armies are led by God to slaughter entire cities of men, women, and children. Sometimes, the Almighty does the gruesome job all by Himself. (Being as more than a few of the women would have been pregnant, that makes God a most prolific killer of fetuses.)

Murder

An Israelite male brings a foreign woman into his tent for a bit of lovemaking. Unfortunately, he is spied by a fellow named Phinehas, who sneaks in with a spear and pierces both man and woman "through her body." (She must have been on top.) As a reward for committing this double murder, Phinehas is given a "covenant of peace" and his descendants are granted "perpetual priesthood." [Num 25:6-13]

Without any sense of a wrong being committed, the Bible's authors tell of this incident in the life of the prophet Elisha. He was walking to Bethel when "some small boys came out of the city and jeered at him saying, `Go up, you baldhead!' And he turned around, and when he saw them, he cursed them in the name of the Lord. And two she-bears came out of the woods and tore forty-two of the boys." [2Kings 2:23-24]

Thievery

The Lord commands people to ask their kind neighbors for loans of money and jewelry, and instructs them not to repay.

Adultery

Having more than one sexual partner was both an acceptable and admired state for Jewish men, especially royals – king Solomon supposedly (exhaustively) enjoyed the favors of some 300 wives in addition to his harem of 700. [1Kings 11:3] Soldiers were encouraged — without regard for their own marital status — to take the virginity of feminine conquests.

The bringer of what came to be known as "Mosaic Law" was a man who often practiced, encouraged, and ordered murder, thievery, and rape — and then blamed his actions on his god.

And so, it is clear that the rules against killing, stealing, and adultery were only meant to protect the property of Jewish men. These, and the rest of the so-called Ten Commandments were never intended to be applied universally. Therefore, it is disingenuous, at best, to use "Thy shalt not kill" as a rallying cry against abortions, capital punishment, or war — none of which are in conflict with biblical values.

Betrayal

A king lusts for the wife of one of his soldiers, so he has that soldier abandoned at the battlefront where he is sure to be killed. Then the king rapes the woman. All of which does nothing to tarnish his reputation among the Hebrews as a great king.

Sex Trafficking

A man passes his wife off as his sister and profits greatly when the king adds her to his harem. Years later, the husband pimps her again to another ruler. This slime-ball is now honored as the father of the Hebrew nation!

Another man offers his own virgin daughters to a large crowd for their carnal sport, simply to save his reputation for hospitality. He is touted as the most moral man in his city.

Repression of Women

Females are property, first of their fathers and then of their husbands. Not only are they not allowed to vote, they are not even counted as citizens. The only opinions they may voice are those of their mates.

Intolerance of Dissent

All authority over others is granted by God. Those who defy any leader's God-given authority are to be killed;

this includes citizens who defy their government and children who defy their parents.

Justification of Slavery

The enslavement of foreigners is a common practice, supported by divine decree. No biblical character — in either testament — ever suggests otherwise. Throughout the centuries since, the Bible has often been quoted in defense of slavery.

Nepotism

The organization established by Moses has become the envy of every tyrant, to wit:

- Only the Levite tribe could come near the holy tent.
- Only Aaron and his sons could enter the tent and commune with God.
- The other tribes of Israel had to support the Levites.
- Only Moses heard God announce these rules.
- Moses was a Levite. Aaron was Moses' brother. Any questions?

Racial Discrimination

"You shall not eat anything that dies of itself; you may give it to the alien who is within your towns, that he may eat it, or you may sell it to a foreigner; for you are a people holy to the Lord." [Deut 14:21]

And so, virtually every conceivable crime and dastardly act is not only described, but honored, within the pages of this purportedly holy book. On close examination it turns out that "Biblical Values" are the opposite of those needed in any civilized society.

Lie #9: "It's a sin to speak with spirits."

Although intermittent and often tenuous, from our very beginnings there have been communications between folks in the physical world and spirits in other realms. While it is true that some spirits do not have our best interests at heart, most who manage to make contact try to communicate the truth to the best of their understanding. (Living in a different dimension by no means imparts omniscience.)

Prohibitions against spirit contacts are founded more on priests protecting their turf, than on any concern for the sources being demonic. Beyond their encouragement of painful persecutions, such self-serving injunctions qualify for this book because they have prevented great quantities of wisdom from being imparted to, or being accepted by, us Earthbound souls.

Some people have concerns about sitting with a medium or consulting a psychic because they think that doing so puts them at odds with certain teachings in the Bible. The main support for this belief in the Old Testament is from the book known as Leviticus. The key verse (generally labeled 19:31) says, "Do not turn to mediums or wizards, do not seek them out to be defiled by them."

There is another verse in Leviticus and one in Deuteronomy that clearly judge those who make a practice of talking to dead people: "A man or woman who is a medium or a wizard shall be put to death;" and "There shall not be found among you any one who … is a medium [for they are] an abomination to the Lord."[64]

There can be no doubt that these statements are in the Bible and that they distinctly prohibit consultations with the spirit world. If you accept Leviticus and Deuteronomy as the inerrant word of the Almighty, then you would be wise to avoid any contact with mediums or psychics. But, before you make such a decision, you might want to know what else you are signing on for. There are numerous other things that are likewise prohibited by these ancient writings.

Have you ever eaten a rare steak? Or a fatty hamburger? Have you ever trimmed your hair or beard? Did you ever get a tattoo; peek at a sibling in the nude; fail to stand when an old man enters the room? Have you ever worn a shirt of cotton and polyester blend? Perhaps you have been upset with the government and cursed a politician? According to the Old Testament,[65] all of these acts and many others are sins against the Lord and are condemned just as strongly as consulting a medium.

And if you actually *are* a medium, do you deserve to die? These books say you do. But they also condemn you to immediate execution if you ever had an affair with a neighbor, or used withdrawal as a form of birth control, or had a homosexual encounter.[66] Think you're safe because you never went in for such hanky-panky? Well, did you ever happen to get angry with mom or dad and curse them or disobey them?[67] According to the Old Testament, if you've done any of these things, you are already just as doomed as you would be if you helped someone converse with their dear departed grandmother.

Why and how the Old Testament came to have such pernicious laws is too long a story to tell here. Suffice it to say that it is a tale of nepotism and greed beyond what any big-city politician would dare emulate today. No matter the rationale, though, there is no authority in selectively citing passages that support your point of view while blatantly violating or completely ignoring scores of other definite rules clearly laid down by the same priesthood. For the sake of this chapter, I am going to assume that the reader would agree with me that being stoned to death is not an appropriate penalty for disobeying one's parents. (Although as a parent I have sometimes wavered in that view, I admit that I wouldn't be here to write this if such a law had been in force during my own teenage rebellions.) Most reasonable people will likewise find the bulk of these Old Testament strictures to be overly harsh, if not abhorrent. If you can be comfortable getting your hair cut, then you should have no qualms about visiting mediums or accepting the value of their words.

Another, less direct, argument against mediumship is that dead people cannot talk, therefore all communications are actually with demons who are trying to deceive the living and lead them away from God's word. The verses most often cited are these from Psalms: "For in death there is no remembrance of thee; in Sheol who can give thee praise?" and "The dead do not praise the Lord nor do any that go down into silence." [Psalms 6:5 & 115:17]

In truth, these are the words of a poet addressing his Creator and imploring Him to "Help me now; Don't wait 'til I'm dead." The author clearly is not God (Would he be composing pleas to himself?) and is not claiming any special knowledge beyond the rather primitive beliefs of his fellow tribesmen. Besides, these exhortations could just as easily be read to imply that spirits *do* still exist and *are* capable of receiving favors.

Also note that the writers of the Old Testament did not connect the idea of mediums or spirits with either demons or the devil; that idea came along much later.[68] And then there is the matter of "by their fruits you shall know them." If the results of a spirit communication are alleviation of grief, enhanced compassion, reduction of anxiety, a feeling of being closer to The Almighty, and other such positive feelings and actions, then what role could the devil be playing? What sort of demon goes around encouraging folks to love one another?

Now, this is not to say that all dead people are good people. Experience teaches the opposite; people don't tend to change very much when they die. Nasty folks can thus become nasty spirits. So, it's wise to be cautious, especially when attempting contact on one's own. In more succinct terms: "Test the spirits."

Which leads us to the New Testament.

Nothing in the New Testament admonishes us not to visit mediums or speak with the spirits of departed friends and relatives. Quite the opposite!

The earliest writings in this collection are seven letters written by Paul. (Another seven letters are commonly titled as being Paul's writing, but were likely written by others.[69]) The earliest of these, and thus the earliest known document referencing Jesus, is *First Thessalonians*. In this letter, Paul encourages his readers, "Do not despise prophetic utterances, but bring them all to the test and keep what is good in them and avoid the bad."[70] Paul's next surviving missive is *First Corinthians*, wherein he claims: "In each of us the [Holy] Spirit is manifested in one particular way, for some useful purpose. One man, through the Spirit has … gifts of healing, and another miraculous powers; another has the gift of prophecy, and another the ability to distinguish true spirits from false."[71] And in *1 John*, we are advised, "Do not trust any and every spirit, test the spirits to see whether they are from God."[72]

Such admonishments seem to indicate that early Christians spent much of their time in their meetings making ecstatic utterances and prophesying. The only concern that the apostles had is that their followers may be listening to the wrong spirits. This is a most significant shift from the attitudes expressed in the Old Testament. Previously, anyone who approached the tabernacle without specific authorization would be struck dead by Jehovah Himself. Although a prophet's voice would occasionally be recognized as legitimate — so long as he concentrated on warning the Hebrews to obey Jehovah or face terrible retribution — that's a far cry from encouraging everyman to converse directly with the Almighty. This change of attitude is likely because the early Christians had no entrenched priesthood that jealously guarded their exclusive (and highly profitable) rights to divine contact.

Testing the Spirits

Spirit contacts should be validated using two criteria: (1) source, and (2) intent.

We all have subconscious minds which store vast quantities of information, much of it not immediately available during our normal waking moments. This seemingly unknown information may be transmitted to our conscious awareness in the form of gut feelings, simple knowingness, interior voices, or even by drawing attention to ambient objects. (This latter could be noticing a new pattern or curious activity; even picking a particular book from a shelf.) Any such messages can easily be mistaken for spirit contact.

Another mis-identified source can be an awareness of the thoughts of other people. Mental telepathy is not fictional; although it is rare and has never been proven to communicate lengthy messages accurately.

It is tough to be certain that messages purportedly emanating from the spirit realms are not the result of subconscious memories or mind reading. Verification of facts that you would otherwise have no way of knowing can provide confidence in the source. Otherwise, you are left to rely on your gut instinct.

The second part of testing the spirits is determining their intent. There is no Devil, but there are demons, that is, there are souls who get pleasure of sorts from attempting to influence us to our detriment. Any self-proclaimed spirit who berates the living, advocates violence, encourages unhealthy habits, or teaches fear, automatically fails the test. You can only benefit if you listen exclusively to sources that promote compassion, tolerance, forgiveness, and joy.

Even if you are sure that you are in communication with a well-meaning spirit, keep in mind that physical death does not impart omniscience. People retain much of their false beliefs during their transition, and all heavenly realms are not equal in wisdom.

On the whole, treat spirit communicators with the same courtesy and skepticism you would when speaking to any stranger during normal social intercourse.

Wisdom of Spirits

For those readers not familiar with many spirit teachings, I offer a few brief samples herewith.

★ *"Those who deny us and say we preach the gospel of darkness are in line with the same people who, in the days gone by, made the same accusation against the Nazarene [Jesus]. We come with the same power of the Great Spirit, bringing the same manifestations of the spirit, the same message: 'Comfort the mourner, heal the sick, bring light to those who are in darkness, health to the afflicted, strength to the weary, knowledge to the ignorant.' "*[73]

★ *"This is both the goal and the glory of God: that His subjects shall be no more, and that all shall know God not as the unattainable, but as the unavoidable."[74]*

✱ *"If you've got a chance to help, do it. If you've got a chance to reach out, do it. If you've got a chance to love, never pass up the opportunity. … You can't figure it out, and sometimes it's not your place even to begin to try to figure out why they might be creating a tragic reality, but you reach, you love, you care, and there's never a point where you stop."[75]*

✱ *"Some people think journey towards God be sit down, wings sprout out of back, fly around, smile at people, silly smile. Go around, bless people, flap wings, say big revelations. No. No big silly smile, no wings. Just be better people to each other."[76]*

✱ *"We abjure and denounce that most destructive doctrine that faith, belief, assent to dogmatic statements, have power to erase the traces of transgression; that an Earth lifetime of vice and sloth and sin can be wiped away, and the spirit stand purified by a blind acceptance of a belief, of an idea, of a fancy, of a creed. Such teaching has debased more souls than anything else to which we can point."[77]*

✱ *"The individuating consciousness seeks, through the experience of human reality, to know itself fully and completely so that it can return to the Oneness with a greater light and a greater understanding. This adds to the reality of the Oneness."*[78]

Afterword

"It is only when resistance is paralyzed by the agency of superstition, that the race can be subjected to systems of exploitation for hundreds and even thousands of years."
— Upton Sinclair, *The Profits of Religion*, 1917

With the dissolution of the Soviet Union, millions of East Europeans suddenly faced massive changes in their political, cultural, and financial lives. The most wrenching shift was the abrupt re-write of their history. Many people in those traumatized countries still find it difficult to accept that their understanding of political events, their feelings about who were the good guys and who were the bad, their whole sense of how far they had come and the road they had traveled, were all founded on the massive web of lies spun by the gang of despots known as the "communist party."

Most Westerners reacted to the political changes with a mixture of elation and wonder. Many worried that it was only temporary. Some tried to ease the burden of the dislocations. But few thought: "Watch out!

Our turn is coming." After all, we were already enjoying the fruits of democracy and free enterprise.

Now it is everyone else's turn. Now, West Europeans, Africans, Australians, and Americans must face up to the fact that our great religions have long been tools by which politicians steal our money, limit our freedom, and subdue our will. We have been on a steady diet of lies for several thousand years. Now that we have tasted the truth, how many of us will be able to swallow it? And who will choose, instead, to seek security by clinging blindly to the old deceits?

Appendix 1

Notes on Names and Formatting

Typographic Deviations

All quotations are reproduced exactly as spelled and punctuated in the source materials. Quotes from discarnate spirits are preceded by a ✶.

The Names of God

In the Old Testament, the Hebrew name for their tribal god was YHWH, which we pronounce either as "Jehovah" or "Yahweh." Also, Adonai, meaning "Lord," was used to avoid actually speaking the sacred name.

In this book, I use Jehovah to signify the god of the Jews, God (capitalized) to signify the god of Christianity, and some form of The Almighty, Great Spirit, Creator, or Universal Consciousness, to mean the aware matrix in which we humans exist. Divine pronouns are not capitalized.

The Names of Groups

The Semitic people known as Hebrews are the originators of most of the biblical material referenced in this book. As history progressed, they were referred to as Israelites, until they were formed into two kingdoms (Israel and Judah) and the survivors of the latter country became known as Jews. For the sake of simplicity (if not accuracy) I use "Hebrew" in reference to biblical tales and "Jew" as a general term for any follower of Judaism.

Appendix 2
Recommendations for Further Reading

Reality of Psychic Phenomena

The Conscious Universe: The Scientific Truth of Psychic Phenomena, by Dean Radin, 1997.

The Afterlife Experiments, by Gary Schwartz, 2002.

Proof of Spirit Life

The Hereafter Trilogy: The Book That Removes All Doubt, by Miles Edward Allen, 2015.

Life After Death: Living Proof, by Tom Harrison, 2008.

The Articulate Dead, by Michael E. Tymn, 2008.

Description of the Afterlife

The Realities of Heaven: Fifty Spirits Describe Your Future Home, by Miles Edward Allen, 2015.

Heaven and Hell Unveiled, by Stafford Betty, 2014.

Journey of Souls, by Michael Newton, 1994.

God Is Not Great: How Religion Poisons Everything, by Christopher Hitchens, 2007.

America's War on Sex, by Marty Klein, 2012.

The Power Worshippers: Inside the Dangerous Rise of Religious Nationalism, Katherine Stewart, 2020.

One Nation Under God: How Corporate America Invented Christian America, Kevin M. Kruse, 2015.

The Profits of Religion, by Upton Sinclair, 1917.

Appendix 3
Organizations Worthy of Your Support

Americans United for the Separation of Church and
State [AU]
Freedom from Religion Foundation [FFRF]
Planned Parenthood, Inc.
Society for Psychical Research [SPR]
American Civil Liberties Union [ACLU]
Institute of Noetic Sciences [IONS]
Secular Coalition for America
Parapsychological Association [PA]

END NOTES

[1] The remainder of this subsection is essentially copied from *Together Sex*, first published by Grove Press in 1977.

[2] Ryerson, Kevin, and Stephanie Harolde, *Spirit Communication: The Soul's Path*, 1989, p. 172.

[3] Rodegast, Pat and Judith Stanton, *Emmanuel's Book*, 1985, p. 205.

[4] Ward, Suzanne, *Matthew, Tell Me About Heaven*, 2001, pp. 61, 66.

[5] Barham, Martha J., *The Silver Cord*, 1986, p. 62.

[6] Gould, Terry, *The Lifestyle*, 1999, pp. 90, 199.

[7] _________, p. 90.

[8] This includes both the material and the astral realms. See *The Realities of Heaven* for more about intimate relationships in your future homes.

[9] See *America's War on Sex* by Dr. Marty Klein.

[10] The Jews of the time, like many cultures today, were dedicated to maximizing their population and so frowned upon any waste of semen in either masturbation or nocturnal emissions. But, assuming such a "crime" was discovered, designated punishments were fairly mild — executing the perpetrators would have been self-defeating.

[11] Newton, Michael, Ph.D. [a client of] in *Journey of Souls*, p. 142.

[12] Those readers who do not accept this statement as fact will benefit immensely from reading my *Defending Reincarnation*.

[13] The carol *We Three Kings*, written in 1857 for a Christmas pageant at the New York City Theological Seminary, took its characters from a 6th century Latin text that both numbered and named what the Bible simply refers to as an unspecified number of astrologers (or "wise men" in the King James version).

[14] The best-known historian of the time, Josephus, devotes 37 chapters to chronicling Herod's every misstep, both petty and grand. But neither Josephus nor anyone else mentions a slaughter of the infants.

[15] Also: Zoroaster, Krishna, Apollonius, Alcides, Osiris, Hercules, Mars, Vulcan, and Pythagoras.

[16] Spong, John Shelby, *Rescuing the Bible from Fundamentalism*, 1991, p. 16.

17 Klein, Marty, *America's War on Sex*, 2012, p. 22.

18 See "A Sumer Garden" in Lie #5.

19 Pagels, Elaine, *The Origins of Satan*, 1995, p. xvii.

20 Hefner, Hugh, "The Playboy Philosophy, part 1," *Playboy*, December 1962, p.63.

21 Klein, *op cit.*, p. 28.

22 Barham, Martha J. and James T. Greene, *Bridging Two Worlds*, 1981, p. 200.

23 Homewood, Harry, *Thavis Is Here*, 1978, p. 86.

24 Putnam, Allen, ed., *Flashes of Light from the Spirit-Land*, 1872, p. 255.

25 Thibault, Henry, ed., *Letters from the Other Side*, 1919, p.110.

26 Montgomery, Ruth, *A World Beyond*, 1971, p. 64.

27 Borgia, Anthony, *Life in the World Unseen*, 1954, p. 59.

28 Miller, Jr., Walter M, *A Canticle for Leibowitz*, 1964, p. 214.

29 7,405,926 is composed of four prime numbers multiplied together ($2 \times 3 \times 11^2 \times 101^2$).

30 Wetzl, Joseph, translator, *The Bridge Across the River*, written in 1915, published in German in 1950, English translation published in 1973, p. 46.

31 Barker, Elsa, *Letters from the Afterlife* [a.k.a. *Letters from a Living Dead Man*], 1914, p. 247.

32 Austen, A.W. ed., *Teachings of Silver Birch*, 1938, p. 109.

33 Stringfellow, A., *Leslie's Letters to His Mother* — [as quoted in *The Afterlife of Leslie Stringfellow* by Stephen Chism, 2005], 1926, p. 102.

34 Xavier, Francisco Candido (Chico), *Nosso Lar: Life in the Spirit World*, 1944, p. 41.

35 Taylor, Ruth, *Witness from Beyond*, 1975, p. 59.

36 Montgomery, *op. cit.*, p. 126.

37 Sherwood, Jane, *The Country Beyond*, 1969, p. 132.

38 Burbidge, A.H., *The Shadows Lifted from Death*, circa. 1941, p. 146.

39 Boards covered with letters and numbers that could be pointed to with a small triangular table known as a "planchette" or "traveler" were often used by spirit seekers during the early 1880s. On February 10, 1891, Elijah J. Bond was granted the first patent on such a board. His business partner, Charles Kennard gave their version the name "Ouija," which he falsely believed was Egyptian for "luck." Parker Brothers bought the rights to the name in 1966, so I use the generic "talking board" from here on.

40 1 John, 4:1.

41 Gen 1:24-27

42 Gen 2:7, 19-22

43 Gen 9:20-24

44 Gen 3:22

45 Adapted from *Asimov's Guide to the Bible*, pp 21-30.

46 In order to attain the magical number 10, "various Christian bodies have divided them quite differently. Some divided the first commandment about God into (1) You shall have no other Gods and (2) You shall make no graven images. They are identical in meaning. Others divided the last commandment into (1) You shall not covet your neighbor's house and (2) You shall not covet your neighbor's wife. They are obviously two aspects of the same injunction. The number ten, however, served the didactic purpose of teaching." — John Shelby Spong, *Rescuing the Bible from Fundamentalism*, 1991, p. 252.

47 In *Time Enough for Love*, page 352. He goes on to say: "All other 'sins' are invented nonsense. (Hurting yourself is not sinful — just stupid.)"

48 Gow, David, "The Philosophy of Survival," in *Survival*, edited by Sir James Marchant, 1924, p. 140.

49 See Heinlein's *Stranger in a Strange Land* for instance.

50 A more extensive list may be found in chapter eight of *The Realities of Heaven*.

51 Homewood, Harry, *Thavis Is Here*, 1978, p. 37.

52 Knight, J.Z., *Ramtha*, 1986, p. 125.

53 Barham, Martha J. and James T. Greene, *The Silver Cord*, 1986, p. 171.

54 White, Mary B., *Letters From the Other Side*, 1917, p. 37.

55 Swain, Jasper, *Heaven's Gift* (originally published as: *On the Death of My Son*), 1989, p. 61.

56 Puryear, Anne, *Stephen Lives!*, 1992, p. 207.

57 Sherwood, Jane, *The Country Beyond*, 1969, p. 135.

58 White, Stewart Edward, *The Unobstructed Universe*, 1940, p. 241.

59 Duffey, Eliza Bisbee, *Heaven Revised*, 1921, p. 26.

60 The song *Two Out of Three Ain't Bad*, written by Jim Steinman, was recorded in 1977 by the American musician Marvin Lee Aday (whose stage name was Meat Loaf) for his album *Bat Out of Hell*.

61 Available in both print and e-form from Amazon.com.

62 See brief bios of Curran and Xavier at http://www.spiritsatplay.com/Psi-Workers.shtml.

63 For more spirits' descriptions of the next realms see *The Realities of Heaven*.

64 Lev 20:27 and Deut 18:10.

65 Lev 19:26, 3:17, 19:27, 19:28, 20:17, 19:32; 19:19; Ex 22:28.

⁶⁶ Lev 20:10; Gen 38:9; Lev 20:13.

⁶⁷ Levi 20:9; Deut 21:18.

⁶⁸ See Lie #4 for more on Satan.

⁶⁹ These are not exactly examples of plagiarism, but rather have been labeled as letters written "in the tradition of Paul" by early scribes. See: *From Jesus to Christ*, by Paula Fredriksen, Ph.D., 1988.

⁷⁰ I Thessalonians 5:19-20.

⁷¹ I Corinthians 12:8-10.

⁷² 1 John 4:1.

⁷³ The spirit known as Silver Birch via medium Maurice Barbanell, *Teachings of Silver Birch*, ed. A.W. Austen, 1938, p. 83.

⁷⁴ Walsch, Neal Donald, *Conversations with God - Book 1*, 1995, p. 115.

⁷⁵ The spirit known as Lazaris via medium Jach Pursel. *Lazaris Interviews, Book I*, 1988, p. 173.

⁷⁶ The spirit known as Japu via medium Kevin Ryerson, *Spirit Communication: The Soul's Path*, Ryerson and Harolde, 1989, p. 270.

⁷⁷ The spirit known as Rector via medium William Stainton Moses. *Spirit Teachings*, 1883, p. 55.

⁷⁸ The spirit known as Emmanuel via medium Pat Rodegast. *Emmanuel's Book*, co-ed. Judith Stanton, 1985, p. 39.

9 781699 046128